CREATING

QUALITY

MEETINGS

Richard I. Winwood

CREATING

QUALITY

MEETINGS

Latest Techniques for Mastering Group Communication

Richard I. Winwood

Foreword by Hyrum W. Smith

Franklin International Institute, Inc.

Franklin International Institute, Inc.
P.O. Box 25127
Salt Lake City, Utah 84125-0127

Printed in the United States of America

2 3 4 5 6 7 8 9 10
ISBN 0-939817-08-X

To my grandfather,
Edward Amil Enz.
He was a Swiss immigrant in the 1880s who
logged in the forests of the
Pacific Northwest, owned a small
ranch in west-central Washington, and
retired driving a school bus.

He was one of the greatest men
I have ever known.
To my knowledge,
he never attended a meeting
in his entire life.

Contents

Foreword

Not long ago I flew from Utah to New York City to attend a meeting at a very prestigious company. (If I told you the name, you'd recognize it!) This particular meeting was to resolve an extremely important issue relating to the company and how it would position itself in future marketplaces. As it turned out, this was the third of several meetings on the subject. My role in the meeting was as an outside resource—an expert witness, if you will—on how training could be used to change corporate culture and provide strategic direction.

There were thirteen people in the meeting, all high-paid executives. Each participant seemed anxious to arrive at a solution, and each had an idea or two to contribute. However, after five full hours of discussion, politicking, hidden agenda presentations, and numerous interruptions, the meeting was recessed to a day two weeks in the future. Some progress had been made but not as much as I would have expected from such a gathering. In fact, as I boarded my return flight, I wondered if more problems had not been created by that meeting than were solved.

After my in-flight meal, I reached into my briefcase and pulled out a manuscript that Dick Winwood had asked me to review. By the time I was through the first few pages, I realized that I had a whole series of recommendations to make to my client company—not on training solutions but on the process of conducting and participating in effective meetings. As I read on, more and more ideas were expressed that had direct bearing, real "in-your-face" stuff on improving group communications, defining objectives, and reaching consensus, principles that could have been used to great advantage in the experience I had had only hours before.

I don't know how many books there are on how to run a meeting. I've tried to read a couple of them, but I always got bogged down in complex technicalities that seemed to distort the issue—as if meetings were more important than the purposes for which they were called. Not this book. This book is down-to-earth, practical, and immediately applicable. Dick has a gift of expression that makes it delightful to learn about a discipline that most of us consider a necessary evil. As you read it, you'll find yourself saying, "I wish I had read this book ten years ago!" I wish I had.

Dick has researched the subject in depth and combined that research with years of personal experience. He has surveyed thousands of business leaders to get their views and perspectives on meeting effectiveness. It's all in here. Not in complicated theories, formulas, and systems, but in easy-to-learn principles; principles that will have tremendous practical impact on those smart enough to learn them and apply them.

HYRUM W. SMITH
Chairman of the Board
Franklin International Institute, Inc.

Acknowledgments

I owe my gratitude to many people in the making of this book. Among them are R. Dean Herrington, my hero in meeting management; Phillip E. Bozek, a mere genius in group facilitation; and Gerreld L. Pulsipher, a wizard in the art of communicating. I deeply appreciate and acknowledge the assistance of Robert F. Bennett. His help on the manuscript was indispensable.

Thanks also to Valerie Ahart who did a superb job of analyzing and documenting the meeting effectiveness survey. I greatly acknowledge Linda Allen who acted as chief editor for the book. My assistant, Carol A. Force, was characteristically outstanding. She contributed much to the flow of the book and, as usual, makes me look better than I really am.

I want to thank collectively all of my colleagues at Franklin and all the training professionals at our client companies who contributed to the technique and ideas presented here.

Finally, I extend my love and deep appreciation to my wife, Judy, and to each of my children. Their support, encouragement, and love sustain me.

A meeting is nothing less than
the medium through which
managerial work is performed.
That means we should not be
fighting their very existence,
but rather using the time spent in
them as efficiently as possible.

Andrew S. Grove
High Output Management

1

In this chapter . . .

While nearly everyone in the world attends meetings of one kind or another, most people consider meetings major time-wasters and even avoid them if at all possible. However, meetings are a vital management tool and a key component of organizational success. In order for meetings to be effective, leaders and participants alike must understand and apply correct principles of group productivity.

Meetings 101

Everybody meets. Staffs meet, project managers meet, new employees meet, teachers meet, ball teams meet, church groups meet, families meet, neighbors meet. Everybody meets. There is probably not a single activity more common to the day-to-day running of millions of diverse organizations around the world than the practice of holding and participating in meetings.

I don't know how they got the information, but some experts on the subject have calculated that over eleven million meetings are held each day in the United States alone. Another source I read recently suggested the real number is sixteen million! With all these meetings going on, you would think that meetings are the most popular and productive way for people to spend their time—until you ask them!

Trying to find an average meeting goer who will give a good report about meeting effectiveness would give Diogenes a whole new mission.

One book I read stated flatly that most managers consider the meetings they attend to be only 25 percent effective. I've taught hundreds of time management seminars over the last eight years and have observed that seminar participants invariably identify meetings as major time robbers.

It has become culturally acceptable to browbeat meetings. In most companies, meetings are considered a necessary evil—something to be avoided at all costs—but, like the weather, they are seemingly beyond the control of mortals.

Not so, say I. Some meetings are as exciting as others are boring; some are as productive as others are a waste of time; some are as organized as others are chaotic.

Meetings are like any other vital management discipline. Used correctly, they are a key component of organizational success. It is only when they are used incorrectly that meetings become the problem instead of the solution. They *can* be controlled.

How?

This book was written to answer that question. I find that what most people know about planning for, conducting, and participating in meetings they learned on the job. As a result, their success (or lack of it) *in* meetings is not apt to be any better than their range of experience *with* meetings. For most managers, learning to use meetings effectively is a case of the blind leading you know who. There are no business school courses titled *Meetings 101*.

I am always a bit amused when I read yet another mini-research report, usually tucked neatly into a corner of a business periodical, which states something like, "Seventy-two percent of all managers in the U.S. think meetings are a major time waster." Beneath these inane statements of editorial dandruff is the name of some research group you never heard of, right? I want to ask, "How did you define 'meeting' to these 72 percent?" Personally, I think 72 percent of all those surveyed didn't understand the question.

The confusion could be eliminated by clearly defining what is meant by the word "meeting." Here is the meaning of the word as it will be used in this book:

A meeting is a gathering of two or more people for the purpose of reaching a common objective.

It's that simple, really.

A meeting can be:

- A boss and a secretary sitting at a single desk reviewing the events of the upcoming day and coordinating tasks, appointments, and assignments

- Three engineers gathered at the production line reviewing the workings of a new process installed to enhance materials-flow in a distribution center

- Twelve whatever sitting in a conference room, complete with white board, overhead projector and tape recorder, discussing whatever

- Sixty-five sales people on-line in a single telephone conference call learning and asking questions about a change in corporate organizational structure

- A formal session of a board of directors, with a legal secretary taking the minutes

The scope of meetings, in terms of variety and complexity, is enormous. Meetings constitute a management tool that can be applied in a kaleidoscope of ways—anticipating and solving problems, gathering information, finding alternatives, defining opportunities, building relationships, or just having fun.

However, it is when we lose sight of our basic definition of meetings that we lose sight of their purposes and objectives. With such losses, productive meetings are difficult or, more often, impossible to achieve.

It is no wonder that after sitting through a few ill-conceived and malpracticed meetings one might very well adopt the attitude that "meetings are a waste of time." But, when appropriately planned for and conducted, meetings can be the best use of time. Before giving up on meetings altogether, consider the following points.

Facts about Meetings

1. *Meetings Are a Reality to Be Dealt With.*

Aside from whatever bad experiences or emotional baggage you may bring to this discussion about meetings, you will still have to attend them. In fact, the average forty-five-year-old middle manager in corporate America will spend approximately seventeen thousand hours in business meetings in the next twenty years. Meetings are a part of reaching organizational as well as personal objectives. They are a part (a very important part!) of business life. Meetings happen. It's a fact.

2. *Meetings Are Conducted and Attended Amid Environmental and Organizational Constraints*

It would be great if all conditions relating to meetings could be perfect — like our plans. We can wish for it and even do our part but, in the end, rooms will sometimes be too crowded or too hot or too cold; meeting participants will arrive later than expected; interruptions will occur; agendas will not be prepared or will not be followed appropriately; consensus will not always be reached. Overhead projectors, slide machines, and other meeting paraphernalia will sometimes fail at precisely the wrong time. It may not be fair, but it's the way it is. It's a good idea to remind yourself periodically that our objective is to produce a quality meeting experience — not to reach some unattainable perfection. Prepare,

prepare, prepare, then go with the flow.

3. *Meetings Are Not Always Necessary;*
   They Can Be Ineffective and Costly.

Meetings are no panacea. Trying to use a screwdriver as a hammer (or vice-versa) can be an extremely unproductive and frustrating experience for a carpenter, even though both are vital tools of his trade. Likewise, holding a meeting when another medium of communication would be more effective and then blaming the resulting inefficiency and waste on the meeting rather than the decision to hold it is like blaming a screwdriver for not being an effective hammer.

Return on Investment (ROI)

Nearly everyone understands the ROI issue — particularly when dealing with personal or organizational finances. We instinctively seek for the greatest return with the least amount of risk in whatever investments we make. So why not consider the meetings you plan for and conduct as an investment? Meetings are an investment in a very real sense. An investment in time, space, and direct expenses is being made every time a meeting is held. Accordingly, there should be

a direct and obvious return on that investment. And, just as obviously, if there is no significant return identified, then perhaps the
meeting should not be held.

How do you determine ROI for your next
meeting? As you begin thinking about a
meeting to solve a problem, consider the
simple questions that follow and do a quick
calculation.

A. How many people will attend the
meeting?

B. What is the approximate, average,
direct hourly cost (salary, benefits,
etc.) per participant?

C. How long (in hours) do you expect your
meeting to last?

Once you have this data, you can easily
calculate the direct meeting costs:

$$\textbf{A x B x C = Direct Costs}$$

Is it worth it? Can your meeting provide a
reasonable return on investment based on the
direct costs?

I find it interesting that few executives
can, by their signature alone, purchase a
piece of office equipment or furniture. Usually
several levels of approval are required. (After
all, we have a need to control capital costs.)
Most managers can, however, call meetings of

several key people and use tremendous amounts of time and money with no approval at all, and many times with no results.

In addition to direct costs in meetings, there are other significant costs involved. There are often emotional or psychological costs that ripple through an organization as a result of some meetings that have an even greater impact on organizational productivity.

A meeting is obviously a management tool to be used wisely.

What Goes Wrong In Meetings?

With the assumptions about meetings we've just reviewed, it is easy to see that meetings can have problems — even the best meetings could be improved in some minor area. When embarking on a meeting, we may find ourselves in the middle of a meeting mine field with a vast array of explosives hidden just beneath the surface.

Have a look at the list of meeting problems that follows. Even a novice at meeting attendance could identify a few problems he or she has experienced. Review the list and see if you can identify the three problems that have the most negative impact on the meetings you attend.

- Leader out of control
- Participants late in arriving
- Meetings start late
- Meetings end late
- Poor visual aids
- No agenda
- No results or follow-up
- Side issues predominate
- Room too hot/cold/cramped/noisy
- Key people late in arriving
- Unrealistic expectations
- Objective unclear
- Interruptions/distractions
- Agenda not followed
- Meeting unnecessary
- Dominating personalities
- Lack of preparation

- Too many participants
- Poor attitude/personal relations

Did you select your three? Quite a few others have done this exercise with some interesting results.

During the summer of 1990, thousands of meeting surveys were distributed to people in various organizations across the United States. Of over three thousand responses, one-thousand nine-hundred and thirty-four were found to contain enough information to meet research needs. The survey form (page 140, figure B) asked respondents to consider four different categories of business meetings they attend in an average week and to esti-mate both the number of hours involved in each category and the percent of meeting time they felt was productive. They were also asked to indicate the three most significant meeting problems they encountered in meetings they attend. The list of meeting problems was the same as you have just reviewed.

Overall results showed that a significant amount of time spent in meetings was consid-ered "wasted" — up to 64.6 percent! Effective-ness varied, however, depending on the cate-gory of meeting being considered.

MEETING TYPE:

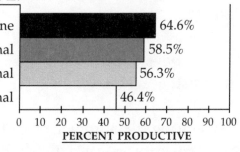

PERCENT PRODUCTIVE

Of the nineteen possible meeting problems, survey respondents selected the following six most often, in the order shown:

1. Side issues predominate
2. No results/follow-up
3. Objectives unclear
4. Lack of preparation
5. Meetings end late
6. No agenda

A complete research report can be found in the Appendix.

Analyzing the research data proved an interesting and insightful experience.

Profession, industry, management level, sex, company size, zip code, you name it — it didn't seem to matter what group or subgroup was involved in the survey, the results were nearly identical. In fact, I had the survey data sorted and tabulated in as many ways as I thought meaningful, looking for some combination that would give me a different distribution of meeting problems. No dice. Moreover, in Time Effective Meeting seminars I've taught since the survey, participants indicated meeting problems that are in concert with survey results. Case closed.

Since most of the meeting problems identified fall into such a narrow span it makes solving the problems, or at least identifying possible solutions, that much easier. And, even if you identified meeting problems that were different than the survey results, determining how you can reduce or eliminate the problems will provide you and your organization with a significant return. When you consider that the average middle manager judges the best of meetings to be only 65 percent effective and yet participates in over seventeen hours of meetings per week, the opportunity for improvement is rich indeed.

Also, while it's good to have a clear picture of the problems faced in today's business meetings — and, particularly those most common in your organization — keep in mind that meetings are necessary and important. Don't fight them. Don't downplay their significance. Look for ways to improve effectiveness and efficiency in the meetings you attend. Have quality meeting experiences.

The Quality Meeting

Quality meetings begin with understanding what a meeting really is, making sure that a meeting is the necessary tool for reaching the objective at hand, and then applying techniques and skills that will help make the meeting a time-saving, effective experience.

To do this, it helps to understand basic meeting elements and how these elements can be combined to help you achieve your team objectives. That is the focus of chapters two through five.

In these chapters we will be working through the **Quality Meeting Model**, beginning with **Roles** (What part will people need to play in the meeting to make it optimally productive?), **Types** (What variety of meeting will best meet the meeting need?), and **Methods** (How should the meeting be conducted?). At the core is the **Meeting Plan** (How to bring these basic elements together into a "power agenda").

Quality meetings are the result of a carefully planned balance between meeting Roles,

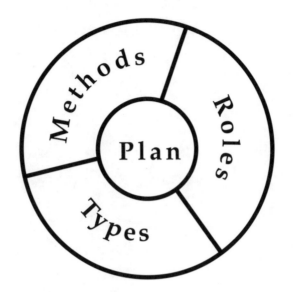

Types, and Methods. In the next chapter we will begin our study of the Quality Meeting Model by investigating the various people roles that are available to help us reach meeting objectives. People are the key exponent of effective meetings. It is people that "make" a meeting — people working together toward a common objective.

A management team will never function effectively in its meetings unless
all members learn to carry out certain
important functions and assume
certain responsibilities.

Dr. Thomas Gordon
Leader Effectiveness Training

2

In this chapter . . .

Meetings are more successful when the correct people participate within assigned or assumed roles. Meeting leader, participant, recorder, etc., each play an important part in reaching the group objective. Here are specific definitions and guidelines for essential meeting roles.

Meeting Roles

A Meeting Is a Stage

Well, not exactly. However, when people who are involved in meetings each understand and fulfill the responsibilities or roles they have in reaching the objectives of the meeting, productivity in meetings can soar.

During the course of a meeting, there are many roles filled by each person involved. Some members will fill just one, while others have multiple responsibilities. We will focus on the key roles of facilitator, meeting leader or chairperson, recorder, time keeper or expeditor and, of course, member or participant.

The Facilitator

The role of facilitator, in my judgment, is the most difficult meeting role to fill well. The main reason is because this person must remain neutral. No small task, especially when the subject is controversial or emotional — as many are. Since no one is truly neutral, this role must be given to or assumed by one with mighty thickness of skin and skills in communication.

The facilitator does not contribute directly to the *substance* of the meeting, only to the *process*. In a way, a facilitator orchestrates the other meeting roles toward the objective. Perhaps "traffic cop" is a better analogy. ("Whoa! Henry, let's go in order here. We'll start with Dennis, then to Colleen, Shirley, and back to you, Henry.")

Additionally, the facilitator defends every person in the meeting and their contributions from personal attack, if required. He will draw out feelings and sugges- tions from each member to ensure orderly participation. ("Debbie, Bob has made a suggestion in good faith, what suggestion or idea can you add?")

At the same time, the facilitator can be blunt, if

necessary, confronting antagonistic or disruptive members. ("Lynn, you seem to not want the group to succeed. Is there a problem?" "Dick and Carol, you two don't seem to be participating much; what are your concerns?")

Through it all, the facilitator should provide positive feedback and encouragement. ("Great question! Now we're really moving. Thank you, Lisa.")

Facilitators are rarely used, in my experience. Most meetings have a meeting leader who controls the flow of the meeting while being an active participant in helping to reach objectives. Situations which call for facilitation are those where neutrality is an asset, as when there is conflict within the group which must be overcome to reach a meeting goal or when the conflict resolution *is* the goal. In such cases, the facilitator is commonly a consultant who is either from outside the organization or far enough removed from the conflict to remain impartial.

Typical techniques of facilitation include:

- Clearly defining the meeting objective
- Explaining the facilitator role
- Encouraging participation of members
- Giving information to clarify details
- Making sure each member idea is heard

- Returning questions to the group
- Building group-esteem
- Helping the meeting group to meet their common objective

A facilitator can become a participant in a meeting if she feels the need to contribute an idea. However, she must first gain permission from the group to "remove her neutral hat" for a moment. Meeting participants must know when she moves out of, and back into, the facilitator role. (Example: "Okay, I'm feeling a strong need to get involved at this point. I'm going to drop out of my facilitator role for a moment just to make this point. . . . [The point, idea, clarification, etc., is made.] Thanks. Now, let me return to my neutral position.")

Meeting Leader

Typically, a meeting leader is thought to be the one most responsible for the effectiveness level of the meeting. While it's generally true that the leader shoulders the majority of the responsibility, each role bears its share of the effectiveness burden. The meeting leader role is critical simply because so many of the key decisions and activities of the meeting come under his control.

For example:

- Defining the meeting objective
- Selecting participants
- Designating time and location
- Determining the type and method*
- Preparing the agenda
- Calling or announcing the meeting
- Arranging for all audiovisual equipment
- Conducting the meeting
- Assigning a recorder and time keeper*
- Delegation and follow-up of action items

*To be identified and defined later in the chapter.

The meeting leader may also fill other roles in the meeting, e.g., participant, time keeper, recorder, etc. He often plays the facilitator role, reserving any expression of opinion until everyone else has spoken. However, his major responsibilities are to plan for and conduct meetings to reach planned-for results.

Dealing with Difficult Situations

Meetings, because they involve multiple people and depend on interactions of differing personalities, will inevitably involve situations that will be difficult for a meeting leader. Participants will look to the meeting leader to handle these situations and to preserve meeting effectiveness.

What are the potential problem personalities? There are three general categories involved here:  1) people who are chronically late for meetings, 2) people who talk too much, and 3) those who rarely, if ever, participate verbally. It is the meeting leader who will orchestrate the meeting in a way that will shut one down occasionally and bring the other out into the conversation.

1. *The latecomer*

This person typically arrives for the

meeting five to fifteen minutes after the announced start time, usually entering the room and taking his place with a flourish of activity and a muttered apology. "Well, where are we?" he might ask. What a guy. Don't feed him the bread of the meeting. Save him the crust—"Hello, John. We're on item three of the agenda and Nancy is just about to give her report. Nancy?"

Always starting your meeting on time is the best way to impose a discipline on late-comers. Even at that, if a member of your routine meeting is chronically late, try a kind but firm comment to him after the meeting adjourns. He'll most likely get the point. "John, it would help both of us if you could be at our meeting when it starts. It seems you've been coming in later every time. Is there a problem I should know about?"

2.   *The dominating personality*

This individual has a comment to make on nearly every point; the self-proclaimed expert on most subjects. ("Lucky you, here I am!") Or he could simply be an undermining influence more interested in confusing the leader than in making a decent contribution. In most cases, the rest of the members in the meeting will recognize this person for what he is. As a meeting leader, you should maintain a cool head. If you have to go on the attack, remember to attack the inappropriate behavior and not the individual. First, let him express himself. If comments are made by him that are out of line, you can always say to the group, "Well, we've heard from Vince. How do the rest of you feel?" If that seems too confrontive, I would involve others in the group by asking direct questions to individuals, avoiding the problem personality.

3. *The friendly neighbor*

These folks always have a partner. With the partner, they engage in various forms of verbal and nonverbal behavior that can drive a meeting leader whacko. At times, these side conversations are simply someone trying out an idea on a fellow member, in which case the discussion should be short and sweet. If it turns into a meeting within a meeting, you'll have to act. First I would try some direct eye contact. If that doesn't work, I suggest a direct attack—not unkind, but to the point. "Hey, guys. We can only have one conversation going on at once here. Please?" or "Phyllis, do you and Harry have something to share with the group?"

4.   *The unassertive, silent member*

Many people have great fear of speaking in front of or even as a part of a group. The cause of this anxiety is usually inexperience, or shyness brought on by fear of embarrassment. If you sense that you have such an individual in your meeting, you could help them overcome their timidity by asking a question of them that they are sure to be confident in answering correctly. It helps to bring them in and make them feel a part of the group. Such an icebreaker can help them to become a more valuable member. You may even set it up by telling them before the meeting that you will plan to ask them such and such a question. No one need know that it was a set-up. Give this person as much encouragement as you can. As a meeting leader, one of your responsibilities is to train your meeting members in how to participate if necessary.

There are lots of other problem personalities, more than I can document because there are so many shades and variables involved. There are, however, two things for the meeting leader to keep in mind. Remembering and applying these two simple ideas will help you to avoid conflicts with problem personalities.

You lead the meeting. All participants are aware when you are out of control because of a problem personality. Use the agenda as a disciplining agent first, then rely on your authority as leader. Be appropriate and kind but never let others take control of your meeting.

Be sensitive to meeting participants. Uninterested behavior may be a signal that your meeting is not relevant to a particular member; perhaps you are not making the experience as interesting or as participative as it could be. If you think this may be the root of the problem, don't hesitate to sincerely ask for a quick and honest evaluation of the meeting before you adjourn. People will help, if they can and if they are asked, to improve your meetings. It's always tough to take constructive criticism, but if you can maintain a level of teachableness you'll come out way ahead.

The Recorder

The recorder is selected by the meeting leader and has responsibility for recording the meeting memory. Unless it is a formal legal proceeding, the recorder takes "selective

notes," not a detailed transcript. Particularly, the recorder codifies key information regarding:

1. Disposition of agenda items
2. Delegated tasks
3. Decisions reached

Insofar as is practical, the meeting record (or minutes) should be recorded in such a way that all participants can see them as they are written, as on a black/white board or, preferably, on an easel-mounted flip chart. When all participants see the record as it is taken, they are better able and usually more willing to edit or clarify when necessary. ("John, I think we agreed that the inventory report was to be submitted on March 15th, not February 15th.")

When using a flip chart (I think you really have to have one of these for meeting memories), you can pin or tape tablet pages to the wall of the meeting room as the minutes develop. It makes it easier for the meeting leader to review each agenda item and reach group closure or summarize meeting products by simply referring to notes that all can see.

Following are samples of flip chart style pages with meeting notes. Notice that these examples use an "outline" format. I got this idea from Andrew Grove, CEO of Intel Corporation, in his book *High Output Management*. Mr. Grove says that outline notes are easier to follow because major points are quickly recognizable. I have used this technique ever since I read Grove's book and I highly recommend it.

How we are perceived in community on Social Issues:

1. Affirm Action —
   Poor — Need to i.d. more unrepresented groups

2. Flood Control —
   Public unaware of responsibility
   • identify potential flood areas
   • hold regional public meetings

3. Uplift Program —
   Educate public on benefits

> Encourage Employees
> To Participate:
> 1. Nancy N. – Do empl.
> record search –
> report 11-7
> 2. Have engineering
> i.d. flood plan –
> maps, etc.
> Sched. 1st mtg. by 11-10
> 3. Hold til Dec. mtg.

Another, more right-brained, approach to thought construction and note taking is the use of mind-mapping. The mind-mapping technique is especially useful when constructing a group project or ideas with a common base. For example, let's say you were holding a meeting to plan the various aspects of the company picnic. The common or root issue is the picnic. Subtopics like time, place, food, entertainment, games, program, etc., all need to be developed and assigned as a part of a plan. Using a flip-chart or white-board:

- Print your focus idea in a circle or box in the center of the page.

- Print key ideas or thoughts on lines connected to the center focus.

- First branches are key ideas, related ideas are connected as sub-branches.

- Print key words only.

- Use color to stimulate and organize if appropriate.

- Show connections and groupings.

The advantage of the mind-map is that ideas can be added easily to an overall scheme

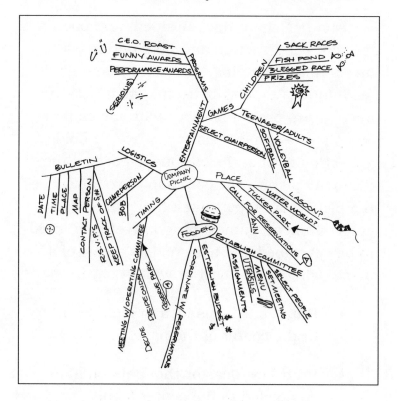

without the disruption such an addition would cause in a linear list. Once all the necessary information has been added to the map, branches can be isolated and formal lists can be drawn up and delegated.

The role of recorder requires certain skills of listening, questioning (for clarity), interpretation, and the ability to write so that others can read. The recorder can be someone who will have no other role in the meeting, but often, for reasons of practicality, the recorder is also a meeting participant.

The Time Keeper

This is a simple, but vital role. The time keeper's job is to foster time awareness with the meeting group. Periodically, and informally, the time keeper informs the group of how much time remains for the agenda item being considered or for the entire meeting. If time has run out and if adjustments need to be made, the meeting leader can take appropriate action. The time keeper keeps meetings on schedule. It is a role and a technique that works like magic. Never have a time-limited meeting without a time keeper. Never.

Time keepers should be assigned by the meeting leader, usually at the beginning of the meeting. (If not, the meeting leader becomes the timekeeper, by default.)

"Sarah, will you be our time keeper?"

"Of course, Steve. When should the meeting adjourn?"

"No later than 11:30."

"Fine. We have fifty-four minutes left."

Periodically during the meeting Sarah will softly but clearly say, "We have thirty minutes." "We have ten minutes." etc.

If, as a meeting leader, you simply begin having an assigned time keeper in every meeting you conduct, you will notice a significant decrease in the time you spend in meetings and an increase in meeting productivity.

The Participant

The participant or group member is, of course, vital to reaching meeting objectives. One of the marks of an effective meeting is the extent to which group members actually participate in the process by asking questions and making appropriate comments. While such activity is largely a function of the meeting leader's ability to draw some people into the discussions and to "shut down" more verbose members for a time, if each participant is well aware of the topics to be discussed, prepares to make a contribution and arrives on time, this role will be effective even without a strong meeting leader. Furthermore, if something is not clear, or if support cannot be given to a recommendation, it is the participant's responsibility to speak up! If someone is in error on a factual matter, it should be pointed out.

Participants are invited to meetings because they have some direct presentation to make, an important perspective on the subjects to be discussed, or simply to be informed. They should prepare for each meeting by having all relevant material available for review and by taking appropriate personal notes during the meeting, particularly for remembering important points and follow-up tasks. I suggest that personal notes take roughly the same form as the group memory; specifically, succinct and selective notes taken in outline form. Following is an example of personal meeting notes. The asterisks to the right of text indicate tasks where specific action is required.

MONTH _Apr_ YEAR _92_

DAILY RECORD OF EVENTS DATE _14_

① Jan Watson — Accent on Travel

  a. Can leave for Athens on Sat — but must pay $245 extra. Talk with Sarah; Tuesday okay? ✻

  b. Conf. # for Hermes Hotel — 5467541 — Clerk "Toula"

  c. Need deposit by May 1st.

② Sam Jones, Purchasing meeting ✻

  a. Send May fcst. by Today @ 4 pm.

  b. Prepare for 8-12 meeting. Need 1993 forecast — problem / def. wants overheads plus hard copy. Bring Henry. ✻

③ Dan Edgar — Trix Consulting.

  a. Has idea regarding recycling paper in dist. center.

  b. Appt. set for 5-17 @ 9 am (1 hr.) ✻

  c. Can Jake come? ✻

Specific Meeting Roles

While the roles of facilitator, leader, recorder, time keeper, and participant are vital to most meeting successes, they are general in nature. Within these roles there are, obviously, many other "characters" or functions that contribute to meeting effectiveness. For example, some will provide strategic perspectives, some technical expertise, others bring financial, legal, personnel, or other special information. You can gain insight into the specific roles you will need in your meeting by a quick review of your meeting objective and then considering the type of meeting you will be conducting. In the next chapter we will investigate many different meeting types.

**A meeting is not just a meeting;
there are different types.**

Michael Doyle and David Straus
How to Make Meetings Work

3

In this chapter . . .

Meetings come in many different flavors. Some meetings are routine, regularly scheduled; others are one-time emergencies, called on the spur of the moment. One meeting will simply be assembled to gather or share information, while the product of another is a decision or consensus. Then, there are an unlimited number of variations where meeting types are combined to produce the desired result. Meeting types are part of the "tool kit" of the meeting planner.

Meeting Types

It is obvious that a meeting held to gather information to be analyzed later will be quite a different meeting than one convened to reach a decision or to evaluate a project already in process. Also, there's the regularly scheduled meeting—staff meeting, for example—as opposed to the ad hoc, unscheduled, decision-producing meeting. Interestingly, most of us only know how to plan and conduct one type of meeting—it's "just a meeting." Consequently, meetings often fail to meet objectives effectively because we try to force a meeting type that does not expedite our cause. In effect, establishing the meeting type answers the question: "What kind of a meeting is this?"

The time to clarify the meeting type is not after the meeting is underway, but when the meeting is anticipated. The key to determining the appropriate meeting type may be in the question: "What, generally, do we want to gain as a result of this meeting?" or "What is the desired end product of this meeting?"

As the specific purpose of the meeting comes into focus, meeting types, or combinations of meeting types may suggest themselves.

Have you ever gone to a meeting with one expectation of its purpose to find not only that your perceptions were wrong but also that you were not properly prepared and failed to bring important information? Clearly, everyone invited to attend a meeting should be informed of its purpose well in advance. It is just as important that meeting participants know what type of meeting they are attending as it is to know the time, location, etc.

Generally, there are two different types of meetings—"routine" or "emergency."

The Routine Meeting

The routine meeting is most concerned with the process of something. It is regularly scheduled and participants know what to expect in terms of standard agenda items, meeting format, etc. These meetings, because of their regularity, have little impact on projects and other scheduled tasks on which the participants are working. Typical of such meetings are most staff meetings, sales meetings, project update meetings, operating committee meetings, etc.

The Emergency Meeting

Emergency meetings are ad hoc, designed to produce a decision or solution relative to a sudden and unexpected problem or opportunity. The phrase "emergency" means that the meeting usually has a specific short-term mission and will probably not be as carefully planned as a routine meeting (there may not be enough lead time). Above everything, emergency meetings should be conducted by a meeting leader who has a clear picture of the emergency situation to be considered. Also, keep in mind that emergency meetings are disruptive to projects and schedules of participants—an important consideration when choosing common participants. Keep emergency meetings as lean, peoplewise, as you can. As Andrew Grove says, "Decision Making is not a spectator sport."

Within these two general categories of meetings, there are many other types. The following is an examination of a few of the most common.

Information-Sharing Meetings

These are called anytime you want to gain or give information quickly from a relatively large group—say eight people to several hundred people. Typical applications include: company update meetings (all employees in the cafeteria), product introduction meetings (we're going to preview the spring line), project update meetings, general PTA meetings, etc. Also, a subset type of the information-sharing meeting is the problem-definition meeting. Sometimes the purpose of the meeting will simply be to gain an understanding of the details or scope of a problem, before proceeding to the problem-solving and decision-making process (which may or may not involve another meeting).

The Problem-Solving Meeting

A change needs to be made. For example:

- Short-term business slowdown is anticipated and there needs to be an adaptation in inventory levels.

- You have just become aware of a major opportunity for your company to expand into the European marketplace—several division heads could be impacted.

- You'll be moving to a new building shortly; what is the best way to effect the move for computer and telephone systems?

- Operating budget allocations will be significantly reduced for the coming fiscal year. Where should we start?

The problem-solving meeting should be specifically focused on a problem, as stated above, and geared to work out several alternative solutions. Under most circumstances, participants should be given as much information and time prior to beginning this meeting as possible to familiarize themselves with the situation and to personally evaluate solutions.

The Decision-Making Meeting

Here we evaluate alternatives (which came from the problem solvers, or some other outside source) and try to reach a consensus on which will best meet the need. If there is a wide difference of opinions represented as to what the ultimate solution should be, this can be an interesting task indeed. The word "consensus" is usually assumed, mistakenly, to mean that all participants are in agreement. Actually, according to Webster, consensus is simply having a majority of participants in agreement, yet all willing to support an idea or course of action. I choose Webster's definition because I think it most clearly describes the appropriate usage as far as meetings are concerned. There are important benefits in going the consensus route if you have the time and the need to consider the validity of every alternative, but if consensus isn't necessary or even appropriate to the decision being made, things can move very quickly. You can either simply take a vote or, if you are in a hierarchical organization, discuss it until the decision maker (one person or a small committee) announces the choice. Once the decision(s) has been reached, your meeting should be adjourned or you should move on to the planning or strategizing phase.

The Planning Meeting

Planning is nothing more than bringing future events into the present where proper controls can be applied. Therefore, the planning meeting is where we concern ourselves with implementation of our decision. This is where strategy is determined. Who will do what and when? How will it be done? What deadlines must be met? What's the "critical path"? These are decisions, of course, but they take place in the framework of constructing an overall plan.

This planning meeting is typically where broad delegation of tasks takes place.

Delegation is another simple management discipline that runs amuck much of the time. Since meetings are nothing more than group communication, delegation is largely a process

of intelligent communication between individuals in a group regarding a task or process to be done. Let's review a few basic principles of delegation that should be applied in meetings:

1. Make sure the delegatee clearly understands the scope and specifics of the delegated tasks and projects and has the skills to carry them out. All delegated project tasks should be written!
2. Within what time frames are results expected? Everyone involved should write these down in their personal notes.
3. Authority goes with the job. Give delegatees the tools needed to perform, then stay out of the way unless close supervision is really necessary.

4. Responsibility rests with the delegator. Specific follow-up dates should be agreed upon if the task deadline is more than a week or so in the future.

Ask yourself, "Did everyone write down their responsibilities, deadlines, reporting structure, resources?"

Write everything down. After the meeting, if any participant has to ask "Who was doing the promotion?" or "Which department is bringing salad?" you may have big problems.

Since planning meetings are the platform from which significant effort and resources are mobilized and launched, it is doubly important that every participant keeps notes. Everyone knows.

The Evaluation Meeting

Evaluation meetings are the guardians of the project or developing process. They are held to evaluate progress, work out previously unanticipated problems, and to coordinate/correlate efforts. At the conclusion of a program or project it is a good idea to conduct an evaluation meeting to debrief the experience, celebrate or mourn results, and document successes and problems so that future, like kinds of projects, may benefit. Evaluation can and should be a part of every meeting experience.

Type-Combination Meetings

Some meetings will necessarily contain many meeting types. For example, a meeting could be held to gather information about a situation or problem. Once the information is "in," problem analysis/solving could begin, followed by decision making, planning, etc.

In other, more complex situations, several meetings may be needed to gather information or find alternatives to reaching objectives.

If you are the meeting leader in a type-combination meeting, you will want to clearly communicate when you are "shifting gears" to a new meeting type.

"All right. I think we now have a clear picture of the problem. Let's move on to consider some approaches we can take to solve it."

Combining Types with Methods

Meeting planning and execution becomes exciting when we can design meetings using type/method combinations that truly produce the best result. But a discussion of meeting types gives you only half the picture. Let's meet the other half: Meeting Methods.

Several meeting methods are available to help reach meeting objectives. In selecting a method, the meeting planner should consider the meeting type and purpose, then select the best method to meet those needs.

4

In this chapter . . .

Just as there are different types of meetings, there are different ways, or methods, of conducting them. Some meeting objectives call for a method that helps bring the desired result to fruition quickly and easily. In the following pages, we will discuss some basic meeting methods and how we can use each, or combinations of each, to bring about more successful group experiences.

Essential Meeting Methods

If meeting types answer the "what" question, meeting methods answer the question: "*How* will this meeting be conducted?" By "conducted" I mean the format, layout, and flow that will be used in the meeting to help the meeting accomplish its objective.

I've titled this chapter "Essential Meeting Methods" because there are so many different techniques and variations of methods and new ideas for group communication are being created all the time. Also keep in mind that there are many techniques and "sub-methods" within a meeting. Consequently, because of the numerous variables involved, it's fair to say that no two meetings are alike. Accordingly, in this chapter I will suggest a basic foundation in meeting methodology and let you use your creativity and style as you plan and conduct your own meetings. Following are the main methods by which we structure meetings.

Guided Discussions

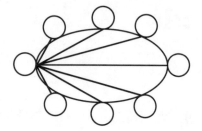

When most people think of a typical business meeting, they envision a small group of five to ten people sitting in a standard conference room. A leader or chairperson is conducting, usually sitting or standing at the end of the table. An agenda is being followed.

Such a meeting represents, more or less, the format of a meeting method called a guided discussion. Probably the reason that this method comes to mind quickest is that it is the most common meeting method in use. I'm guessing for sure, but I would estimate that 80 percent of all business meetings are conducted using this format. For good reason.

Guided discussions have a broad range of application. They are typical to most staff meetings, weekly sales meetings, project meetings, committee meetings, etc. Meetings conducted in this method characteristically have these attributes:

- A meeting leader who conducts the meeting

- A predetermined agenda or meeting plan
- Closure is reached on each agenda item before moving on
- A specific time period

Since most of your meetings will be guided discussions, this method will be assumed when making statements about meetings in general. I'll try to make an obvious distinction when describing or recommending any other method.

Round-Robin Method

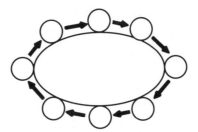

Round-robin meetings suggest a rotating discussion that is used almost exclusively to gather or share information. This meeting method promotes involvement from all participants by giving a "time slice" for reporting to each person—usually from three to five minutes. It is not uncommon to have meeting participants who talk too much—those who seem to comment on every point. You also know people who are very reluctant to participate and contribute in a group setting. The round-robin meeting method helps to solve both problems by limiting the talker to a time slice and compelling the less verbose to join in.

Round-robin can be used as a stand-alone method, but is more commonly used before or within a guided discussion. For example, you may want to begin a meeting by asking participants to introduce themselves in a particular way, starting at one end of the table and going around from there. Or, perhaps you would like to get quick input from a meeting group regarding their feelings about a specific subject before moving on to a more formal guided discussion or brainstorm. If so, using the same "round-the-room" approach can be very effective.

"Let's do a quick round-robin about your feelings regarding the 401K plan performance. Each person should take less than three minutes so let's be as brief as possible. We'll start with Jay and move around to the left. Jay?"

The Brainstorm

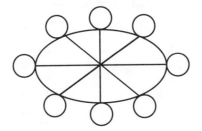

Brainstorming is a structured, usually verbal, solution-seeking meeting method. The purpose behind this meeting method is to generate as many alternative solutions to a given problem or opportunity as possible in a short period of time. Participants express ideas at random, while a recorder writes the ideas for evaluation later.

Brainstorms are typified by creativity and spontaneity; therefore, no critique is offered—positive or negative. The meeting leader should use a facilitation technique when conducting a brainstorm. It is important to encourage participation and manage the process of the brainstorm, then stay out of the way. Imagine a meeting where the leader, using a brainstorming technique, proceeds as follows:

"Okay, now we're going to brainstorm for ten minutes. We need ideas on how we can solve the parking problem in building four.

Ben will write the ideas expressed on the flip chart. Come on, any ideas?"

Sally breaks the ice. "I think we should have parking places according to the size of car each person drives."

"That will never work, Sally," responds the leader. "Surely we can come up with something better than that! Who else has an idea?"

No one has anymore ideas. Imagine that.

There is no quicker way to shut off a creative brainstorming session than to make a critical statement about a suggestion. In this case, Sally's idea may not be implementable or practical, but a related idea, spawned by Sally's, may be a great solution. Let ideas flow without interruption.

At the same time, don't overly praise ideas either. Why? Because, in order to be fair, you will have to give the same approval to every idea. Also, after the brainstorm, when critical evaluation is necessary, an idea receiving praise in the brainstorming session may have to be discarded for a variety of reasons. The person contributing the idea could be offended. "What do you mean it won't work? Shirley said it was a great idea!" Praise participation—not specific ideas.

Above all, encourage creativity, welcoming even outlandish suggestions as a way of generating ideas. Brainstorming should be an exciting, often fun, always productive method.

I would limit brainstorms to no more than twenty to twenty-five minutes. If you're the leader, you will probably sense when the last "kernel has popped," and that's the time to move on. You should now shift into a more traditional meeting format where the ideas can be categorized, prioritized, and evaluated.

Remember, brainstorms don't have to be verbal. In fact, one of the most effective meetings I ever attended was what I call a "silent brainstorm." Here's how it works:

If you have more than seven people, split them into two equal groups and have them sit around a table where they are a bit closer than arms length. Six or seven people to a table is ideal but four or five will work fine. Now, give each member a small stack of index cards and a pen or pencil. Also, it's a good idea to have extra pens and pencils available on each table in case one breaks. (One always does.)

Explain to the group(s) that they will have x number of minutes (usually fifteen to twenty) to complete an exercise in brainstorming. Tell them in detail what problem or opportunity you would like them to focus on for the time allotted. Encourage creativity.

When you say the word, the clock starts and the brainstorm begins.

When a participant has an idea, they jot it down on a card (one idea per card) and pass the card (silently) toward the person sitting to the left. They should then get on with another idea to write down and pass as they did the first.

As the meeting goes on, each participant should have a few cards starting to accumulate on their right. These should be picked up and reviewed (not criticized or praised). If they can add to the idea, they should write the addition on the card with the original. If it sparks a new idea, that new idea should be written on a new index card and passed to the person on the left. Once you've read a card from another member, it should be passed to the left as well (silently). Thus, the cards are constantly going around the table generating additions and new ideas. The only sounds are pencils writing and brains working. It's a hoot!

Once your silent brainstorm is over, you can accumulate the cards and treat the ideas in the same way you would with a standard brainstorm.

The One-on-One

In our meeting productivity survey reported in chapter one, respondents ranked one-on-one meetings as the most effective method—one-on-one meetings were 64.92 percent effective for them. Perhaps it's because this method only involves two people, eye to eye. The conversation, however, can go on much longer than there is something pro-

ductive to discuss unless the participants are disciplined and focused. From a dynamics standpoint, these meetings are usually satisfying simply because each person has an opportunity to express themselves and be heard.

In business, the typical one-on-one meeting involves either a subordinate and a supervisor or manager, or two equals communicating across lateral organizational lines. Here the manager gives the subordinate a chance to address areas of interest and concern directly to his or her direct supervisor. Obviously, the subordinate should bring the main agenda items to the meeting.

The Progress Interview (PI) One-on-One

In addition to being a meeting method, a progress interview is also a wonderfully effective management technique. Just as in more formal (and more populated) meetings, one-on-ones need to be well planned with missions, objectives, and expectations clear to both parties. It's a good idea for both parties to agree not only on what is to be accomplished, but also on what time frames are in order. Note taking is important and results and assignments should be clearly defined before adjournment.

This PI one-on-one is very informal and open. It is a chance for a subordinate to give needed feedback and focus on items of interest and importance. The manager can also have agenda items, but the subordinate's list goes first. (The items often will be nearly the same anyway.)

If you are a manager, holding regular PI one-on-one meetings with each subordinate can be one of the most effective management tools you will ever use.

Another point about progress interview one-on-ones. Can you imagine the impact on family life in the United States if each parent met with each child on a monthly basis (or more often—weekly) for a PI one-on-one? Where the child supplies the agenda? How about a husband and wife where each supplies an agenda and they take turns going first? Save your notes and agendas. In time, I believe, you could write a book on successful family life.

The "Hit and Run" Meeting

Most one-on-one meetings begin with an interruption. In other words, they are spontaneous and unscheduled events. To economize everyone's time, these meetings should be deliberate and highly focused. Beware of the interrupter who strolls in and asks "How ya doin?" or "Yagotta minute?" An effective response is to ask for an "agenda"; get this person to the point! "I'm fine. What can I do for you?" or "Hi, Fred. Can I help you with something?" If you fail to get a specific response, excuse yourself from the conversation as quickly as you can. "Gee, I'm up against a deadline here. Let's meet for lunch or something." On the other hand, if the interrupter has a specific request—"Well, I need to see you about the new vacation policy. Does that start now or at the first of the year?"— answer the question as appropriately as possible and get on with the task at hand. Make it a "hit and run" meeting.

If you find yourself in the role of interrupter, always tell the person you are interrupting what you want and how long you think it will take—and do it right up front. "Jerry, excuse me. I need to see you for about ten minutes about the Williamson report. Is now a good time for you?" Remember to estimate the time you will need, then stick to it.

Everyone should know what to
expect before coming to a meeting.
You must be explicit about what's
going to happen, how the
meeting is going to be run,
who is to play what roles . . .

Doyle and Straus
How to Make Meetings Work

5

In this chapter . . .

As in so many of life's events, a little planning up front can save countless hours and many problems in execution. In these pages, we will learn the principles of planning for successful meetings — whether to hold a meeting or not, how to prepare an effective agenda, and even how to announce your meeting.

The Meeting Plan

Michael LeBoeuf, author of *Working Smart,* wrote "Working smart in meetings is much like the rest of life—an investment of time and energy in forethought and planning pays handsome dividends." I like that. I like the idea of taking time, even if only a few precious minutes, to carefully plan for a meeting. Crawford Greenewalt, former president of DuPont, once observed that effective managers were those who took the time to plan out activities first, then work through their plans at a relaxed, rather than frantic, pace. He said, "Every moment spent planning saves three or four in execution." Meeting planning can produce multipliers of productivity much higher than three or four times!

Hold 'Em or Fold 'Em

Before we plunge headlong into planning for a meeting, let me stop first to tell you about an idea I heard once that would help a person read fifty thousand words per minute. Yes, fifty thousand. The suggestion was to find a potentially interesting book. Read the table of contents and briefly glance through the text. Then, decide *not* to read it.

Now, let me tell you how to hold a two-hour meeting in five minutes. Look over the proposed agenda, consider the objective, alternatives, the people and the expense involved, and decide not to hold the meeting.

Why? As I mentioned in chapter one, meetings are not a panacea. (There are meetings that die of old age that never should have been born.) For example, meetings are often not good tools when there is much anger or anxiety in the group. Meetings sometimes are a management ritual—held because "We've always had a Monday morning meeting." A meeting may be an act of cowardice held only to put off making a difficult decision. Be honest with yourself. Also, if you've already made up your mind about a particular subject and can't be swayed, don't have a meeting to make it look like you're being participative. (You could hold a meeting to explain and communicate, but that's different.)

For regular, scheduled meetings, ask yourself what happened the last time you held this meeting. Was there follow-up? How well did your group work together? Was it fun? Did something productive happen as a result? Was it worth the trouble (ROI)? If not, maybe the meeting doesn't pass the test; cancel it.

If your meeting does pass the test, continue on with your plan.

I am amazed at how often people attend meetings for no other reason than that they are invited. It is not uncommon at all to drag ourselves off to meetings with only the foggiest idea as to the objective, topics under discussion, our personal roles or responsibilities, etc. If you are the meeting leader, it is your task to make sure these questions, and many others, are answered as soon as practical prior to your meeting. If you are asked to attend a meeting as a participant, you have a certain right to know what it is all about and how you should prepare.

For a meeting leader, the agenda is where the meeting initially takes form and ultimately provides the meeting discipline. For the participant, a detailed agenda answers the needful questions poised above.

Planning is the most important—even vital—part of meeting leadership. Unfortunately, planning is the most neglected activity in meeting leadership. Don't make the mistake of thinking that you do not have time to plan and communicate before your meeting—95 percent of the time it isn't so. Also, the result of conducting a meeting without an appropriate level of planning simply means poor meeting results. You *don't* have time for that!

The Agenda

An agenda is your meeting plan. It is the principle means by which participants learn content, objectives, and process. It is the principle tool for the meeting leader to use in meeting control. Agendas are not a "nice" thing to have in a meeting—they are a *vital* tool for time-effective meetings.

Your agenda should detail all important information about:

- Why the meeting is being held (your prime objective).
- What is going to happen (meeting flow).
- Who is going to do what (role definition).
- Where the meeting is being held (specific location).
- When the meeting will start and end (time frame).

On the opposite page is a meeting planning form that accomplishes the needs of a standard agenda in a "fill in the blanks" format. The nice thing about using such a form is that it encourages the meeting leader to consider all important aspects of the meeting plan. In fact, just the exercise of filling out this form can be an excellent means of meeting preparation. Another advantage of the form is simply that it takes so little time.

MEETING PLANNER

Date Scheduled _____
Meeting Title _____
Purpose _____
Desired Results _____
Location _____

Scheduled Time			Actual Time			Meeting Costs
Start	Stop	Total Hrs.	Start	Stop	Total Hrs.	

Meeting Method _____ Meeting Type _____
Facilitator _____ Recorder _____
Group Leader _____ Time Keeper _____

Group Members To Attend	Attn.	Value Per Hr	Total
1			
2			
3			
4			
5			
6			
7			
8			
9			
10			

Items To Be Discussed	(Sequence)	#
1		
2		
3		
4		
5		
6		
7		
8		
9		
10		
11		
12		
13		
14		
15		
16		
17		
18		

Form # 4022

This form shouldn't be too intimidating (it's hardly a 1040). Let's do a quick run-through to familiarize you with each entry slot:

1. *Date Scheduled.* Here's a novel idea. Let's tell each participant exactly when the meeting will start and the latest it will be adjourned.

Keep in mind that most meetings lasting more than one and one-half hours start to reach the point of "diminishing returns." You can go beyond that time frame, of course, but you would do well to schedule a break or exercise every hour and a half or so.

2. *Meeting Title.* A title should tell the participants something about the meeting and give the meeting some identity.

3. *Purpose.* A simple statement of mission. For example: Coordinate activities, plan for the charity ball, receive project reports, elect officers, etc.

4. *Desired Results.* What you would like to have accomplished by the time your scheduled stop-time is reached. What do you want to happen as a result of this meeting?

5. *Location.* Make sure you include the building number or name, the number and name of the meeting room, and directions on how to get there if necessary (a map?).

6. *Scheduled Time.* Tell everyone when you will start and stop the meeting. Seems simple, but most people can't estimate how long it will take to accomplish a group objective very accurately—one gets better with practice, but it's always wise to overestimate rather than underestimate the time needed.

7. *Actual Time.* To be filled out after the meeting to show how closely you estimated time requirements. This may seem a trifle rudimentary, but it can be a great evaluation tool for a meeting leader.

8. *Meeting Cost.* We all know that meetings can cost enormous amounts of money. The total cost of daily business meetings in the United States runs into the billions of dollars. Billions. Your meeting will be one of them. Simply take time to consider the cost of holding the meeting and the benefit derived. Obviously, the benefit should far outweigh the cost.

A simple way of determining direct people cost is to multiply the number of people in your meeting by their approximate average hourly wage, times the number of hours in the meeting. I did just that in a recent operating committee meeting I attended. The cost of that meeting was $680 per hour. That meeting better be very productive or very short.

9. *Method, Type, and Role Assignments.*

Here's where you can specify these elements. Do you see how having to fill in these blanks can get you thinking about important aspects of your future meeting? That's the idea.

10. *Group Members to Attend.* List the participants. As you do so, keep in mind that, generally, the more people you invite to the meeting, the less effective the meeting will be. Generally again, I think the meeting begins to lose effectiveness when there are more than eight people actively involved. Choose carefully. Make sure that each participant can make a significant contribution. If you think of someone who could help on one or two points, or give insight to a particular problem or opportunity, perhaps you could call them or visit them briefly, get their input and report for them in the meeting. You could always ask such a person to send you a brief memo outlining their views. Believe me, a person who has the option of giving you a few bits of information, or even sending a short memo, instead of attending a meeting—will feel honored. It's a simple question: "Nancy, I'm conducting a meeting next Thursday where we will decide the location of the distribution center. It won't be necessary for you to attend the meeting, but I know you have some thoughts on the subject. Will you send me a short memo with your ideas?"

Material and Preparation Needed *(Number Each Item)*	Person Responsible

Delegated Tasks	

Meeting Notes

© 1990 Franklin International Institute, Inc.

You may have just made Nancy's day.

11. *Items to Be Discussed.* Here's where you can list your agenda items—usually in order. You should show specific item assignments here if you can—see the sample form.

On the reverse side of the form there are spaces provided for additional information vital to the meeting plan, execution, and follow-up. The space titles speak for themselves. See the preceding page.

When You Don't Have a Prepared Agenda

There are some meetings that will not require an agenda form or other times when the agenda needs to be made up on the spot, as in the case of an emergency or chance opportunity. If you enter a guided discussion meeting where an agenda hasn't been prepared, you can easily produce a "spontaneous" agenda by simply making a list of topics or issues on a black/white board or flip chart. Then, treat it like a task list—prioritize it and work through the list in order, checking off the items as they are addressed.

In those few instances where an agenda is not needed, make sure participants clearly understand the objectives to be met and the rules for the meeting.

"Thanks for coming on such short notice. I know this is disruptive to your schedules, but I needed your help quickly and thought this would be the most productive way for all of us. Carol has uncovered an opportunity this morning that needs some fast action. Consolidated Foods is on the verge of purchasing a new computer system for warehouse distribution. They will make a decision by Friday. We can get the business if we move fast, but we'll need to have a proposal to them no later than Wednesday afternoon—that gives us two days. Let's make a list of what tasks need to be completed and who should be. . . ."

The Meeting Announcement

Once the meeting is planned and staffed you will need to notify your participants about the meeting. There are a number of options (FAX, voice mail, letter, phone call, etc.), but the most common is the internal memo. The meeting announcement is a detailed narrative of the agenda. Following is a sample meeting announcement in the form of an internal memo. Make a quick review of the content of this sample. (See form at right.)

All the important information is there:

- Meeting leader
- Subject
- Time frame
- Date and exact time
- Purpose stated clearly
- Participant preparation clear
- Audiovisual availability given
- Question/answer request
- Agenda attached(!)

The only important item left out was meeting location. Did you catch that?

MEMO

To: Distribution
From: Lynn Robbins
Date: May 18, 1992
Subject: Meeting on 1993 production requirements

In order to prepare for inventory requirements in 1993, I would like each of you to attend a 90-minute meeting on the subject on May 28th. The meeting will start at exactly 10:30 and should adjourn no later than noon.

The purpose of the meeting will be to gather information from each of you regarding your inventory needs for 1993, and to decide on the best way of manufacturing and warehousing the inventory. Please bring your inventory forecasts along with any supporting documents. Each of you will have ten minutes to present your concerns.

Order of presentation will be the same as the distribution list. The decision-making session will follow your presentations.

Flip-charts, eraser board and an overhead projector will be available in the room.

Please call me at extension 5634 if you have any questions or comments.

Agenda attached.

Meetings don't just "happen"!
Meetings are an ongoing part of
organizational progress.
Consequently, what happens prior
to and, particularly, after a meeting
is more important than what
happens during the meeting.

Arlen B. Crouch

6

In this chapter . . .

Successful meeting experiences start long before the meeting begins and end long after the meeting is over. The next few pages are lists of things to be done by meeting leaders and participants before, during, and after the meeting that will help to foster success in group communication.

Before, During, and After

Even though this chapter is meant to be somewhat of a review, there's some new stuff in here too. What I want to accomplish is something like a mega checklist—a list of things that should be considered by meeting leaders and meeting participants before the meeting happens, while it is happening, and after the meeting is over.

A quick review of these suggestions as you plan for, participate in, or conduct a meeting will give you a significant advantage and ensure a quality meeting experience.

Let's Deal with the Meeting Leader First

Prior to the meeting, the meeting leader should ideally accomplish the following:

- Clearly define the meeting objective.
- Determine that a meeting was the most appropriate medium in reaching the objective.
- Decide which type and method to use in reaching the meeting objective.

- Create an agenda with items logically linked together.
- Invite only those people essential to reaching the meeting objective.
- Arrange for an appropriate meeting location.
- Establish the meeting time based on need and convenience.
- Distribute the agenda prior to the meeting time—ideally a week in advance.
- Arrive well in advance of meeting time to set up and prepare the room and equipment.

During the meeting, the meeting leader should accomplish the following:

- Start on time—exactly on time.
- Begin by restating the objective.
- Assign a time keeper.
- Assign a meeting recorder.
- Use the agenda to control the flow of the meeting.
- Delegate specific projects and tasks appropriately.
- Review all decisions reached and tasks delegated with the group. Make sure you have reached your meeting objective.

- Schedule the next meeting if necessary.
- End on time or early if the objective is reached.

After the meeting, the meeting leader should:

- Evaluate the effectiveness of the meeting, noting points where improvement is necessary.
- Ensure that all participants and other interested parties receive a copy of the meeting memory.
- Follow up on delegated tasks and other assignments.

Now, Let's Consider the Meeting Participant

Prior to the meeting, the invited participant should:

- Study the agenda for this meeting to be familiar with any advanced preparation necessary.
- Review notes from the prior meeting to make sure any delegated tasks are completed.

89

- If there is an unavoidable conflict, let the meeting leader know you will be absent and make arrangements to receive the meeting memory.
- Clear with subordinates and coworkers any unresolved items that may produce an interruption.
- Arrive at the meeting room a minute or two prior to start time. Be ready.

During the meeting, the participant should:

- Ask for clarification on any objective or agenda item that is confusing.
- Stick to the agenda item being discussed.
- Actively participate—if you have something to say, speak up.
- Show courtesy to other members. Don't interrupt or overpower the meeting.
- Take detailed notes on those items that interest you or have specific application to your responsibilities.
- Constantly look for ways to help the meeting move along and reach the stated objective. Be a team player.

After the meeting, the participant should:

- Review all notes for action items.
- Plan for meeting task follow-up.
- Communicate to subordinates any meeting item that would effect them or their projects, confidential items excluded.
- Don't complain about decisions you sustained in the meeting.

You should review these lists periodically. There is much that could and should be added, by you, that can help meetings you run and participate in be more time effective.

While it's not the most important consideration, the place and time in which meetings are conducted can have a significant impact on the success of your efforts.

Dennis R. Webb

7

In this chapter . . .

Have you ever wondered about the best time or place to hold a meeting? This chapter provides some important and useful insight into meeting scheduling and placing. Get prepared for some refreshing ideas.

The Meeting Environment

Just as with roles, types, and methods, there are a host of different considerations for the time at which you hold meetings and the surroundings in which you hold them. Obviously, you may not always have the best location or the best possible timing, but it's a good idea to find the best of both worlds given your alternatives.

When to Hold a Meeting

Conventional wisdom (loosely defined as what "they" think) tells us that meetings should be avoided on Mondays and Fridays, where possible. Also, "they" say, meeting leaders should shy away from early morning meetings because they don't give participants adequate time to prepare. "They" say to plan meetings within the 10 A.M. to 2 P.M. time frame. These are "good" meeting times. A common suggestion according to "them," for keeping meetings to one hour (for example) is to schedule meetings at 11 A.M. or 4 P.M. That way, participants will have a natural sense of urgency to fulfill the meeting demands prior to lunch or quitting time. Sound logical?

Not to me. While there are good and bad meetings, I maintain that there are no "good" or "bad" times to conduct a meeting. The choice of timing should be tied to the objective of the meeting—just as the selection of a type and method are. I maintain that Tuesdays through Thursdays are typically the most *personally* productive times, during which group exercises should be avoided. Moreover, meeting leaders who have to resort to trick start times to foster an urgency of action or to promote short meetings should seriously evaluate their personal effectiveness as planners and conductors of meetings.

A meeting first thing on a Monday or last thing on a Friday afternoon might be exactly what the content of the meeting and timing considerations call for. Some years ago, I worked as a sales representative for a computer services firm in Seattle. My manager, Bob Lodie, often held sales meetings at 7 A.M. on Mondays. We were usually done by 8 A.M. or so, with all of us "fired-up" and ready to start our week. Bob's meetings were well planned, productive, and motivating. As a result, we had a jump on the day and a significant head start on our competition.

Also, it wasn't uncommon for us to have a meeting at 5:30 P.M. on Friday afternoons, primarily for reporting results and coordinating efforts. Again, these were well-timed and well-run meetings. In my recollection, not one of us regretted or resented the timing of these meetings—they fit in well with what we were doing. Partially as a result of these time effective meetings, we received corporate recognition for our achievements.

For us to have held these meetings in the time window suggested by "them" would have meant infringing on the most productive selling time of the week. That clearly would have been inappropriate and unproductive.

So, when should you hold your meeting?

You decide. Look at your calendar, consider the needs of participants, assess the objective of the meeting and plan meeting times that work best for all involved. Here's a few questions that may give you some help:

- What time slots would be most convenient and appropriate for the invited participants? Are there external pressures—deadlines or due dates—that need to be considered?
- What meeting space is available at what times?

- Can you combine the meeting with some other essential activity (e.g. breakfast, lunch, dinner, exercise, etc.)?
  Warning! Conventional wisdom says that meetings combined with eating don't work out too well. I think they work great. I like "Brown Bag" lunches because they come at a time when participants are naturally away from desks and phones and people do not talk with their mouths full. Is there an off-the-wall time you can use as a change of pace to get everyone's attention (e.g., early Saturday morning conference call, 7 A.M. Monday)?

Selecting the Meeting Environment

You can conduct a successful meeting almost anywhere. Very few of the really memorable meeting experiences I have had have been in a standard-issue conference room.

Obviously, when you have need for projection equipment, cumbersome displays, or electronic stuff, you will need to have accommodating power resources. However, if the objectives of the meeting can be met without such meeting "jewelry" you can meet on a bus, boat, park or mountaintop. On top of that, if the meeting objective warrants it, you can haul along a portable generator. (You *can* take it with you!) An unusual meeting environment can have a big impact on memories and outcome. Be creative.

Even when you have to stick pretty much to the standard environment, you can make the meeting different and interesting. Some of my favorite wrinkles are called:

The Stand-up Meeting

As the name implies, this meeting is held

while all participants are standing up. This can't be a two-hour affair, but if you have few agenda items and less than ten people for fifteen minutes or less, it works well. You simply direct everybody into the meeting room and invite them not to sit down. It may seem a bit awkward at first, particularly when taking notes, but so much the better—everyone stays awake and focused on the objective. Also, stand-up meetings don't tend to last longer than is absolutely necessary. When conducting a stand-up meeting, make sure each person attending ("standing in") has a copy of the agenda to follow or, if convenient, you may have participants stand in a semicircle around a flip chart or white board. Two hands are necessary for successful stand-up meetings — participants should be discouraged from bringing coffee cups, etc. Be sure to let participants know in advance that you'll be conducting such a meeting. A typical reaction by meeting leaders and participants after their first stand-up meeting experience is that they are amazed at what can be accomplished in fifteen minutes. That's what we're after.

The Walk-Talk Meeting

In most one-on-one meetings you have tremendous flexibility. You may want to try "walk-talk," typically a one-on-one meeting (obviously) conducted as you walk. "Where" doesn't really matter. You could actually be going somewhere ("Let's walk down to the ice cream store. I'm buying!") or it may be simply a walk around the block. What it allows you to do is create a non-interruptible environment where you can speak freely and take as long as you need to reach the objective—sometimes you'll walk around the block many times! I've used walk-talks on many occasions and have found them extremely effective. For me, it's an obvious method when a straight out face-to-face meeting is too awkward or too confrontive. It seems to take the pressure off a bit when you're walking side by side. Open communication seems easier.

I imagine every parent has had to have a one-on-one meeting with a child where inappropriate behavior is the topic. I've found that kids, as well as adults, respond much better and are less defensive when they can walk-talk with you instead of having a "big person—little person" sit down. For me, it starts by saying something like:

"Well, Steve, I understand you had a little

problem at school today. Why don't we take a little walk and you can tell me about it."

Walk-talks do not have to be one-on-one. Three or four can also have a good meeting experience while walking.

I know of three business partners who live in the same neighborhood who jog together every morning at 5 A.M. The conversations they have as they jog (not run) together save them hours of office time. It's a meeting, folks, and a darn good one.

If you're not into fitness, or the weather is bad, try a "drive-talk." I'm told that many Mafia meetings are held in a moving car, with the radio on—because it's the best and cheapest way to insure privacy. It can be a highly effective setting for some straight shooting (no pun intended).

Conventional Logic

Maybe we've hit on a new "Natural Law" of group communication.

Go against conventional wisdom whenever it's appropriate to meet your meeting objective.

Good, effective meetings can be held at just about any place and time. Be creative and fun, but don't get too carried away or too weird — remember that achieving the meeting objective is more important than time, place, or method.

Many serious mistakes are made when managers fail to understand the effect meeting dynamics have on individuals. As a result, objectives are often reached at the expense of group or individual well-being.

Robert F. Bennett

8

In this chapter . . .

So much has been said about meeting plans and objectives that it is easy to forget the people aspects of creating quality meetings. Whether dealing with individuals as a group or a group as individuals, there are essential needs to be considered to ensure a positive team spirit and a focused, productive effort. This chapter gives some unique ideas for enhancing the vital human resource.

Meeting Meeting Needs

It is obvious that meetings meet needs. The idea of goals and objectives in meeting planning implies realizing a benefit from assembled brainpower. However, decisions and discussions in meetings are often surrounded by controversy and emotion. People, as individuals or common-thinking groups, come to meetings with "hidden agendas" or highly personalized ideas and concepts. They often believe strongly in their approaches and can be easily injured when their expectations are not met or their ideas do not receive consideration or approval. The negative impact on productivity can be enormous as the ripple effect of nonconsensus meeting decisions pass through the organization.

The Task Need

There are three important—even over-reaching—needs that should be considered when planning, conducting, and following up on meeting experiences. The first, and most obvious, is the task need. The task need is simply stated as the objective or goal of the meeting. The meeting is called to meet this need first and foremost. Without the task need, you don't have a reason to hold a meeting.

In chapter six (The Meeting Plan) there is sufficient detail on how to set and communicate meeting goals and objectives. If you don't already have a good grasp of the importance of meeting objectives or a functional understanding of how to apply them, I suggest a quick review of that chapter. For now, I will turn my attention to the less obvious, but extremely important group and individual needs.

Group Needs

Earlier in this chapter, I mentioned the negative effect on productivity that can result from inattention to needs other than the task need. It is important to understand that productivity can be greatly enhanced by understanding and being sensitive to group and individual needs in meetings.

A group of people in a meeting should optimally operate as a team. There are great benefits in fostering a team spirit in meetings. Think of a sports team for example. On any National Basketball Association team, there are different skills that should blend to optimize productivity in scoring points or limiting the point production of the opposing team. When true teamwork is in place, the outcome of the team is greater than the sum of the individual players. That's why the NBA Championship team would always prevail over an NBA All-Star team. Not because the sum of individual skills of the All-Stars is less (in fact the individual skills will always be greater), but because the champs would function as a team. The synergistical effect of teamwork will always carry the day.

Another example:

Ash Samtani is the owner of a tailor shop in Hong Kong. His tailors hold the world record time for producing a quality, personally tailored man's suit from bolt of fabric and spool of thread to finished product. Their time was one hour and fifty-three minutes. The end product was magnificent. How did they do it? "Teamwork!" says Mr. Samtani. "Each of my tailors is a professional. I chose three of them for the competition (appropriate delegation). I did the measurements personally, then I gave my tailors the details of measurement and style (clarified objectives). They combined their talents to complete the task (teamwork)." There are thousands of tailor shops in Hong Kong, but Ash Samtani is one of the most successful. His success isn't necessarily because he has the best tailors in Hong Kong (though he says he does!), but because they know how to work together as a team to produce a superior product. The result: over thirty thousand happy customers—all over the world.

Unlike a basketball team or a trio of tailors working toward a desired end result, meeting groups don't have the advantage of long practice sessions and competitions. Meeting teamwork must be encouraged on-the-job, often with participants who don't view themselves as team members and perhaps don't even meet together on a regularly scheduled basis.

The principles, however, are the same. One effective technique for enhancing teamwork in meetings is what I call "preconsensus."

Preconsensus

Gaining consensus is a natural part of meeting management seminars and books. What is most often meant by "consensus" is having every person in the meeting buy off, on, or give voluntary approval to the decisions reached or the plan presented. Consensus can be the object of a meeting—usually achieved just prior to meeting adjournment.

Let me ask you to consider a new use of consensus in meeting management—preconsensus. That is, having every group participant buy off on the desired end result at the beginning of the meeting before you ever get into the agenda. The question that needs to be answered and understood by every meeting participant is: "What do we, as a group, want to *happen* as a result of this meeting?"

Once participants gain an understanding based on that question, the energies of participants, regardless of hidden agendas or personal priorities, should be focused jointly on the answer. The result of such preconsensus will be a series of decisions, delegated tasks, or valid information that can be productively used long after the meeting has adjourned. In such an environment, the group need is clarified and met.

Without such consensus, we often have a splintered approach, spending time on technicalities of process, infighting, misunderstanding—in short, an out-of-control meeting. The result of such an experience is a loss in productivity and a waste of time and energy that will go far beyond the meeting time itself. Here, group needs are never fully understood.

Individual Need

In his book *Gaining Control*, Robert F. Bennett provides some significant insight into basic human psychological needs. Research has shown that "emotional" needs are extremely powerful and at times even eclipse the physiological needs for food, comfort, and protection. In fact, many emotional disorders lead to tragic physical disorders—even death.

I don't know of anyone who was ever killed by a meeting, but I've been in meetings where injuries were unknowingly and unnecessarily inflicted. If we, both as meeting leaders and participants, can internalize and apply a few basic principles of human understanding in meetings, the positive output of our meetings will intensify.

Let's consider a quick review of basic individual needs from Bennett's book and change the wording to make the needs more applicable in a meeting setting.

Basic Need 1: We Want to Live

Unless you run with an extremely rough crowd, your chances of living through most meetings are pretty good. Meetings are seldom, if ever, life threatening. However, there are situations where emotional well-being can be threatened or you may threaten someone else's position, idea, or approach in a way that is emotionally injurious. This is basic, interpersonal relations stuff to be sure—the message is simply that we should constantly be aware of the effect of our actions and reactions on the self-esteem of meeting participants and the impact on their productivity.

I have witnessed a number of situations where people were offended by casual, mostly innocent comments made in meetings. In nearly every case there was no offense intended—they were simple cases of misunderstanding or misinterpretation. As a meeting leader, you should overtly avoid misleading or double-meaning comments. If you notice or hear that you've offended someone or that a misunderstanding has occurred, move quickly to correct it. Little is lost and much is gained when fences are mended quickly. As a participant, you are always better off to assume no malice if you feel offended or slighted. Typical business meetings are rarely used to criticize personally. Another point is important here, even vital. It's okay to question another meeting participant's ideas, judgments, or decisions. Such actions are even necessary to effective meeting experience. It is seldom, if ever, appropriate to openly question another's motives. Most hard feelings result when our motives, not our data or statements, are questioned.

Basic Need 2:
We Want to Love and Be Loved

"Whoa," you say! How do we meet this need in a meeting? Well, part of loving is being appreciated. A participant is invited to be in a meeting because he or she has a contribution to make—even if only to observe. Expressing sincere appreciation to individuals can go a long way to foster cooperation and productivity. "Thank you for attending our meeting this afternoon. I sincerely appreciate the contributions you've each made," or "Leslie, just wanted to drop you a quick note to say thanks for your presentation at our project meeting yesterday. You really helped me to understand the situation better. Also, your overhead slides were great! Thanks."

Expressing appreciation has to be one of the easiest ways of improving relationships and building people. It helps to meet such a vital individual need. It's a shame that it's so seldom used. Use it.

Basic Need 3: We Want to Feel Important

This one goes along with Basic Need 2, but with a slightly different bent. Here we need to simply use a person's knowledge or experience to help solve a problem or gain clarification. Recognition is the key word.

"I've invited you here today because each of you has some insight into the task at hand. It's a tough problem, but I'm confident that we can solve it, or take a bite out of it, by pooling our talents," or "Jerry, you've had a good deal of experience working with field offices — how do you think we should roll this thing out?"

The message is simple—You are important, I value you, I need your help.

Basic Need 4: We Want Variety

No one wants to be bored. Making a list of all the things people do to keep from being bored could take hours. In meetings, leaders and participants alike can give the experience variety by occasionally changing the how, where, when, and who of meetings. Don't be afraid to be a little weird about meeting trappings. Even while keeping objectives firmly in mind and economizing time in a meeting, there are a zillion ways to add spice. Do something different.

Our ability to communicate reveals,
more than anything else,
our strengths and weaknesses.

Gerreld L. Pulsipher

9

In this chapter . . .

Communication is what happens in meetings. In meetings, ideas are presented, discussed, decided and often acted upon as they are understood and expressed. When problems arise, they are often the result of miscommunication and/or misunderstanding. This chapter deals with the principles of effective communication and how we can apply them in form and technique to improve interaction and comprehension.

Getting Your Message Across

Shep was an old dog and he suffered more each added day he lived. But he was more than just an animal; he was one of the family. We had all grown up with Shep, shared our hopes and dreams with him, and cried our tears to his kind face. The family could see and feel the pain in his eyes, and that was too much—it was time. Dad couldn't do it. So the buck was passed and I was left alone with the inevitable task. I loaded my gun and climbed on my horse. And, just as Shep had done thousands of times before, the old dog followed along. After we had passed over a couple of hills away from the house, I found a place to put him out of his misery. While still on the horse, I took aim as the dog circled down below. I slowly pulled the trigger. The gun fired when the dog crossed in front of the horse; then I suddenly fell to the ground with the horse on top of me. I had shot the horse in the neck! That walk back home was more painful for me than it ever was for old Shep, who followed along behind.

What You "Saw"

The dog you saw in this story was different from the one I saw; the dad, the hills, the house, and the horse were different from the ones I imagined. The point is, we both created images of what happened in this story that were more complete than the words alone could tell. Also, halfway through the story you probably had a clear idea of where the story was going—only to find out it ended somewhere outside your expectations.

> **Communication: "A process by which information is exchanged between individuals through a common system of symbols, signs, or behavior."**

A meeting is 99.44 percent communication. People can process and think by themselves, but communication implies two or more—a meeting. In the dog story above, we each had our own idea about what was being communicated—we all visualized the situation differently, even though the story (the printed symbols) was the same. It will be well worth the effort to think about the "old dog" occasionally when we are about to participate in a meeting, particularly if we are making a presentation or otherwise giving important input. The point should be obvious. Communication is always interpreted differently in some way by every person involved. In order to communicate clearly, we must explain, act, and present clearly, not only our material but our overall objectives as well.

My purpose here is not to get too deeply into communication theory, but rather to offer some simple, basic helps so that our meeting contributions are effectively enhanced. I will admit to not having done much academic research into this subject. Consequently, what I say here I learned from experience—from sitting through presentations given by well-informed, extremely competent professionals. Presentations that were just *awful.*

So I hope what you get here will be practical. I want these to be techniques you can use and even teach to others.

As with so much of what's important to future successes, 75 percent of having an effective meeting presentation comes under the heading of *preparation.* As a result, I can make a bold promise that if you will seriously consider and apply these few ideas as you plan and conduct your meetings, presentations will be not a little more effective, but *lots* more effective.

Organizing Your Presentation

Organizing a presentation is much like organizing a meeting or project—start by knowing what your objective is. Write it down for *you* to read. "My objective is to inform the group about my progress on the Williamson deal" or "I will persuade the Operating Committee to approve a budget increase for a new computer." Note that one sample objective is to inform and the other is to sell an idea or to persuade. Most presentations fall into one or the other category, even though many need to do both. Understand your objective.

Understand your audience. What style will work best with the most influential people involved? Are they "bottom-liners" or will they want all the details? Are they "people" people —will they like to know the human side of your material, or do you want to stick to budget variances?

What is the knowledge level of the group? Will you need to teach them as well as inform or persuade?

Organize Your Thoughts

Once you have a clear idea of your objective and a good idea of what your audience is comprised of, start to organize your thoughts.

Brainstorm yourself by asking "What are the main points I want to get across?" Write them down, then arrange them in a logical way. Once you have main points, annex supporting ideas to each main point. For example:

Now review your supporting ideas with an eye toward developing any appropriate graphics, charts, or other visuals. Are handouts necessary? How detailed should they be? Should handouts be distributed before your presentation, during, or after the presentation is completed?

Next, design a short introduction and develop a brief, summarizing conclusion. If done right, an effective conclusion will come full circle back to the points made in your introduction. "As I began my presentation I mentioned the need to develop. . . ." etc.

Here's a quick review of the key steps in presentation organization:

1. Know your objective.
2. Understand your audience.
3. Brainstorm main point flow.
4. Add supporting ideas.
5. Assess need for visuals and handouts.
6. Develop your introduction and conclusion.

Readying the Room

If you are to make a presentation in some sort of meeting room, take time *before* the meeting to familiarize yourself with the environment you'll be in. Is the lighting adequate? Is any necessary audiovisual equipment in the room (or will it be) at the time of your presentation? Does it work? Do you know how to work it? Are spare bulbs (or whatever) immediately available? How about whiteboard pens, flip chart paper, or other mystic stuff?

It seems so simple — so obvious. But I

have seen zillions of instances where many of the obvious considerations were not considered. The result was meeting delays and ineffectiveness of biblical proportions. All were clearly avoidable.

Presentation Content

Would you like to be a hero? Being a hero in a meeting is easy, fun, and simple. Make your presentation easy to understand, colorful, and short. Conclude before your scheduled conclusion time. Presto, you're a hero.

You may decide to only have available 80 percent of the material needed to fill your allotted time. Wonderful! In nearly every meeting situation I've observed, the presenter severely underestimated the time needed to present his material, thus, throwing the whole meeting schedule out of kilter. You may plan a few extra points that you could use for filler if needed, but always plan to use less time than scheduled.

Presentation Materials

In order to successfully and productively be a hero, you should prepare your presentation so that it is concise and easy to understand. If your subject is necessarily complex or complicated, simplify the concept to meet the needs of the group. Use graphics where possible, simply flow-chart complex processes.

If simplification, color, and graphics are not your bag, find someone to help you. Either that or force yourself to learn a new talent. You can use "clip art" if you can find the right image but drawings or other art type graphics need not be professional quality or covered with cutesy—all you need is a simple way to get your message across. The best help book I've found on communicating with graphics is *Design Yourself!* by Kurt Hanks, Larry Belliston and Dave Edwards. The book is available at some bookstores or by contacting Crisp Publications, Inc., in Los Altos, California.

Use of Slides and Overhead Transparencies

Slides and transparencies are a common media for meeting presentations. They are good, effective tools for the most part because they are easily seen by all and have many options for graphics and color. However, many times they are misused. Here are a couple of important things to remember when using them:

Place the projector in the room in such a way that you, the presenter, are still the center of attention. The best way is to project slightly off to the side—45 degrees or so.

Avoid this arrangement if you can:

This placement works better:

Make sure you have plenty of space to get to the projector to change transparencies or make other adjustments.

Slide Projector/Slides

- Make sure you have something to project slides on to. Sorry if that seems too elementary. It's just that I've seen so many presentations that started with the presenter finding a proper screen, wall or surface to project on. Then focusing begins, etc. A waste of time and effort.

- Know how to operate the projector. Can you reverse to see prior slides? Do you know how to move forward in the cartridge to find a specific slide? Know your equipment as well as you know your stuff.

- Are your slides dark/light enough for the projection screen? Can the room be darkened?

- Make arrangements for a specific person to handle room lights for you. Then, all you need to utter is "lights, please" and they either go off or on depending on the state at the time.

Overhead Slides

- Check your projector beforehand to see that you have necessary clearance to give a good projection. Is the projector working properly? Does it project a clear, distortion-free image?

- Line up a sample slide prior to the meeting so you know how to place slides on the glass. A simple technique is to put a row of masking tape on the bottom edge of the projection glass, then line up the slide perfectly so you have a centered, straight image. Draw a line on the masking tape with a felt tipped pen at the edge of the transparency.

  Once you've done this you won't have to check every time you put a new transparency up to see if it's centered.

- What do your transparency images look like? Transparencies are not good for full printed pages particularly in standard type. The example following would not be a good overhead transparency:

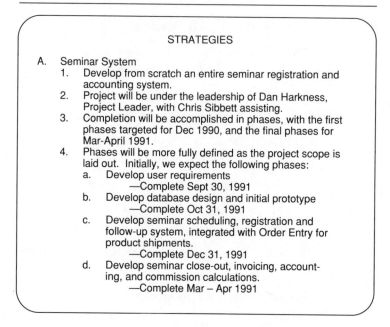

STRATEGIES

A. Seminar System
   1. Develop from scratch an entire seminar registration and accounting system.
   2. Project will be under the leadership of Dan Harkness, Project Leader, with Chris Sibbett assisting.
   3. Completion will be accomplished in phases, with the first phases targeted for Dec 1990, and the final phases for Mar-April 1991.
   4. Phases will be more fully defined as the project scope is laid out. Initially, we expect the following phases:
      a. Develop user requirements
         —Complete Sept 30, 1991
      b. Develop database design and initial prototype
         —Complete Oct 31, 1991
      c. Develop seminar scheduling, registration and follow-up system, integrated with Order Entry for product shipments.
         —Complete Dec 31, 1991
      d. Develop seminar close-out, invoicing, accounting, and commission calculations.
         —Complete Mar – Apr 1991

Here's a better use of the media:

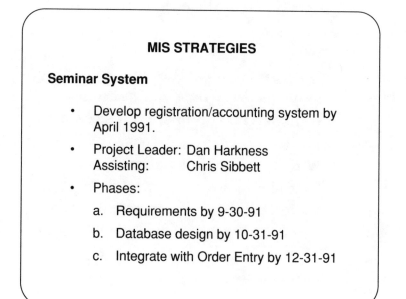

MIS STRATEGIES

Seminar System

- Develop registration/accounting system by April 1991.

- Project Leader: Dan Harkness
  Assisting: Chris Sibbett

- Phases:

   a. Requirements by 9-30-91

   b. Database design by 10-31-91

   c. Integrate with Order Entry by 12-31-91

- Notice the use of bullets rather than detail. The second slide is easy to read and interesting.

- I think it's always helpful to have hard copies of transparencies for each participant. That way, each participant can take appropriate notes right on the copy for reference later.

A common problem for presenters when using projection equipment is remembering to whom the presentation is being given. Have you ever noticed that presenters often focus all their attention on the projected image instead of the audience? When you present, take a glance at the image projected to make sure it's the right one and displayed in the right way, then speak to the group.

One final point on using slides and transparencies. Don't read them to the group. Summarize the information, giving important points, but don't read slide detail. In most cases, participants will understand the printed language well enough to read it themselves.

Questions and Answers

The success of a meeting will often hinge on active participation by all involved. Meaningful participation is often in the form of a discussion about key issues in a free exchange atmosphere—a mutual sharing of ideas. In order to stimulate such interchange (suppose participants look bored, preoccupied, etc.), asking questions can help to refocus the group and clarify what is going on.

Questions typically fall into four types:

1.   *General:* Here you open the floor to a broad range of responses.
2.   *Detail:* These questions focus the group on a specific idea eliciting a narrow range of response.

3. *Group:* These questions call for volunteers to respond.

4. *Individual:* These questions are asked of a selected individual.

Questions

When you ask questions, make sure you are clear as to what kind of a question you're asking. Also, you'll need to be clear as to the question content itself. Don't be passive. A mumbled "Any questions?" doesn't cut it if you want responses. Even with general type questions you can be very open and persuasive in asking for comments or questions. "Alright, before we move on to the next section, I want to make sure I've addressed any questions or concerns you have at this point. What questions do you have?" Now, *wait for a question!* Don't be afraid of silence— people may need a few seconds to review notes for possible questions or to formulate the question itself. If no questions are forthcoming you can say "Gee, I must be a great presenter or you folks are all asleep!—Sure you don't have any questions?"

You can also communicate procedure by simply raising your own hand as you ask, "What questions do you have for me?" You are making an important point—raise your hand when you have a question and I'll recognize you. Participants will follow your lead and not simply call out their questions.

Listening

It is very discouraging for a questioner to get the idea that the person being questioned isn't listening or is disinterested. When a question is being asked, give direct eye contact and really listen. Be relaxed. Process the question in your mind as you receive it. Don't act like you know what the question is before the person asking is finished. Not only is such behavior rude, but you may be surprised to find that you're wrong. Few things are more embarrassing than answering the wrong question in front of a group. Listening is a skill. It is also hard work, if done right. As a listener, you should be sensitive to any underlying issues—you may have to ask yourself, *What is the real question being asked?*

Answering

Luckily, the average person talks at about one hundred words per minute and thinks at over five hundred words per minute. That gives you an advantage as a listener. If someone asks you a complex question that contains two or three points, you can store the information in your mind as point one, point two, etc. Even if the question isn't all that complicated, it's a good idea to restate the question—for two reasons:

1. You gain a clear understanding of the question and the person asking the question verifies the content. It also says, "I listened."
2. In a group setting, everyone can hear the question restated and, therefore, is prepared to receive the answer.

- "Let me restate the question to see if I understand."
- "Before I reply, do you mean that . . .?"
- "Are you asking us to . . . ?"
- "What I heard was . . . Is that right?"

If someone asks a relevant question and you don't know the answer, say so. No apology is necessary. You can simply say, "I don't have the answer to that one yet, but I'll make a note of it and get back to you after the meeting." You can also use a facilitation technique and refer the question to the group. "I don't have the answer to Jim's question. Perhaps one of you has some details on that?"

(Look over the group.) If someone answers satisfactorily, fine. If not, take a note to get back to them after the meeting. Get on to the next question or presentation item.

President Kennedy, when being asked questions in press conferences, used to occasionally preface his answers by saying "I'd like to say this about that. . . ." Then he would respond. It was clear that the President didn't have an immediate answer so he used "prefacing" to give himself a few seconds to formulate an intelligent response. It's obviously best to go directly to the answer if you have it on the "tip of your tongue." If not, a simple "Good question!" gives you a bit of an advantage. If you don't come up with an appropriate answer in the few nanoseconds given you by your comment, go back one paragraph and learn how to say "I don't know."

Finally, don't be afraid to "lighten up" your presentation with humor or amusing examples. A little cartoon or brief situational joke that helps to clarify a point or focus attention on your objective can add to the enjoyment and productivity of any meeting.

Appendix

Meeting Effectiveness Questionnaire

During the spring of 1990, five thousand questionnaires were distributed to business and government people all across the United States. Those receiving the questionnaires were asked to evaluate meetings they attended and to report on the amount of time spent in meetings by configuration, and how productive they felt their meeting experiences were. In addition, they were asked to identify the three most significant problems they faced in the meetings they attended and to give an appropriate amount of organizational and personal information so that significant statistical divisions could be made.

On the next page is a sample of a blank questionnaire. On the following pages are the statistical results.

Meeting Effectiveness Questionnaire

1. Listed below are four meeting configurations which are common in business settings. Please give your best estimate of the number of hours you spend per week in each type of meeting, along with your assessment of the amount of productive time generally spent in each meeting type:

	A One-on-One Meeting (w/secretary, boss, colleague, subordinate, etc.)	**B** Small Group Informal Mtg. (no agenda, problem/ opportunity-related, spontaneous, etc.)	**C** Small Group Formal Meeting (agenda-driven, scheduled, coordinating, reporting, etc.)	**D** Large Group Formal Meeting (boards, committees, correlation, departmental, etc.)
Average number of hours you spend per week in this type of meeting:	hours	hours	hours	hours
Percentage of time in this type of meeting that you consider truly productive:	%	%	%	%

2. In your opinion, what are the three most significant problems with the meetings you attend? (please indicate as 1, 2, 3)

a ＿＿ Leader out of control
b ＿＿ Poor visual aids
c ＿＿ Agenda not followed
d ＿＿ Side issues predominate
e ＿＿ Room too hot/cold/cramped
f ＿＿ Lack of preparation
g ＿＿ Too many particlpants
h ＿＿ Key people late
i ＿＿ Too much socializing
j ＿＿ No minutes
k ＿＿ Late starting

l ＿＿ No agenda
m＿＿ No results/follow-up
n ＿＿ Objectives unclear
o ＿＿ Dominating personalities
p ＿＿ Meeting unnecessary
q ＿＿ Interruptions
r ＿＿ Too long
s ＿＿ Lack of progress
t ＿＿ Poor timing
u ＿＿ Other (please specify):
＿＿＿＿＿＿＿＿＿＿＿＿＿

3. Please indicate the type and size of your organization:

a ＿＿ Manufacturing
b ＿＿ Financial
c ＿＿ Govemmental/Military
d ＿＿ Sales/Marketing
e ＿＿ Educational
f ＿＿ Other:

a ＿＿ 1 to 9 employees
b ＿＿ 10 to 49 employees
c ＿＿ 50 to 249 employees
d ＿＿ 250 to 999 employees
e ＿＿ 1000 to 5000 employees
f ＿＿ Over 5000 employees

4. Please identify your job function: And, a little about yourself:

a ＿＿ Middle Management
b ＿＿ Executive
c ＿＿ Technical/Engineer
d ＿＿ Clerical/Administrative
e ＿＿ Professional
f ＿＿ Other: ＿＿＿＿＿＿＿＿

a ＿＿ Male
b ＿＿ Female

Zip Code: ＿＿＿＿＿＿＿＿＿
Province: ＿＿＿＿＿＿＿＿＿
County: ＿＿＿＿＿＿＿＿＿

Meeting Survey Results

The following report shows the average number of hours spent in four different meeting types, the percentage of productive time spent in these four meeting types, and the most significant problems with meetings attended. This report is based on responses from a total of 1,934 people surveyed.

The results of this survey showed that the meeting type considered most productive was the one-on-one meeting, with 64.6 percent productivity. The least productive was the large-group, formal meeting at only 46.4 percent productivity. The small-group, formal meeting was the next most productive at 58.5 percent. And small-group, informal meetings were 56.3 percent productive.

The top ten most significant problems with meetings overall were as follows:

1. Side issues predominate
2. No results/follow-up
3. Objectives unclear
4. Lack of preparation
5. Too long
6. No agenda
7. Dominating personalities
8. Meeting unnecessary

9. Agenda not followed

10. Too much socializing

The data was then broken up into the following subgroups: job function, size of the organization, and zip code. Following are the results.

Job Function

Middle Management

There was a total of 680 middle managers who responded to the questionnaire. The average number of hours spent in meetings per week by middle managers was 17.9, with the greatest amount spent in one-on-one meetings at 6.8 hours a week. The least amount of time was spent in large-group, formal meetings at only 2.3 hours a week. Of the 6.8 hours a week spent in one-on-one meetings, 65.2 percent were considered productive. Of the 2.3 hours spent in large-group, formal meetings, only 45.9 percent were considered productive. Of the time spent in small-group, formal meetings, 59.4 percent was considered productive, and 59.1 percent of small-group, informal meetings was productive time.

The top five meeting problems for middle managers are as follows:

1. Side issues predominate
2. Objectives unclear
3. No results/follow-up
4. No agenda
5. Key people late

Clerical/Administrative

A total of 212 clerical/administrative people responded to the questionnaire. The percentage of productive time spent in meetings for clerical and administrative personnel is concurrent with those for middle management. One-on-one meetings were considered the most productive with 66.66 percent of the time spent productively. The next most productive meetings were the small-group, formal meetings, with 65 percent of the time spent productively. Small-group, informal meetings and large-group, formal meetings were very close, with 60.93 percent productivity for the small-groups and 60.79 for the large-group meetings.

The five most significant problems for clerical/administrative are as follows:

1. Side issues predominate
2. No results/follow-up
3. Interruptions

4.   Objectives unclear

5.   Late starting, no agenda, meeting unnecessary

Professional

Of the total people surveyed, 372 had professional jobs. These professionals stated that their most time-efficient meetings were one-on-ones, with 61.33 percent of the time used productively. Small-group, formal meetings were next, with 56.67 percent productivity. The third most productive meeting type was the small-group, informal, with 55.49 percent useful time. Finally, the least productive were the large-group formal meetings, with only 44.32 percent of the time being productive.

The five most significant problems for professional workers are as follows:

1.   Side issues predominate

2.   No results/follow-up

3.   Too long

4.   Objectives unclear

5.   Dominating personalities

Company Size

1 to 50 Employees

A total of 457 people worked for a

company with 50 or fewer employees. For this size of organization, one-on-one meetings were the most effective. They considered 63.49 percent of the time spent in these meetings productive. They considered small-group, formal meetings the next most efficient, with 58.18 percent productivity. Small-group, informal meetings were next with 53.53 percent productivity, and large-group, formal meetings were the least productive with only 49.32 percent efficiency.

The five most significant meeting problems for small organizations are as follows:

1. Side issues predominate
2. No results/follow-up
3. Objectives unclear
4. Lack of preparation
5. No agenda

50 to 999 Employees

There was a total of 659 responses from people who worked in organizations of 50 to 999 employees. The midsize organization again found the one-on-one meetings the most productive, with 63.49 percent productivity. However, the midsize company found the small-group, informal meeting, with 57.65 percent efficiency, slightly more effective than the small-group, formal meeting, which had

57.57 percent productive time. The least productive was again the large-group, formal meeting.

The five most significant meeting problems for midsize organizations are as follows:

1. Side issues predominate
2. No results/follow-up
3. Objectives unclear
4. Too long, lack of preparation
5. Dominating personalities

1000+ Employees

Of the total surveyed, 710 worked for organizations with over 1,000 employees. Large organizations also found the one-on-one meetings to be the most useful. They considered 64.75 percent of their time in this type of meeting productive. They considered 59.03 percent of the time spent in small-group, formal meetings productive, and 56.93 percent in small-group, informal meetings. Once again, the least effective was the large-group, formal meetings.

The five most significant problems for large organizations are as follows:

1. Side issues predominate
2. No results/follow-up

3. Objectives unclear
4. Lack of preparation
5. Too long

Zip Codes

Prefixes 0-5

There were 664 people surveyed with a prefix of 0-5. This group found the one-on-one meetings to be most effective, claiming 64.75 percent of the time spent here productive. They considered the next most productive to be the small-group, formal meeting, with 59.03 percent productivity. Small-group, informal meetings were next, with 56.93 percent useful time. Finally, large-group, formal meetings were last with only 45.12 percent productivity.

The five most significant problems for prefixes 0-5 are as follows:

1. Side issues predominate
2. Objectives unclear
3. No results/follow-up
4. Lack of preparation
5. Too long

Prefixes 5-10

Finally, there were 1,100 responses for the prefixes beginning with 5 and ending with

10. These 1,100 respondents once again found the one-on-one meeting to be the most effective, considering 65.14 percent of the time spent here productive. this group then considered the small-group, informal meeting to be the next most effective, with 57.98 percent productive time. Small-group, formal meetings were close behind with 57.79 percent productive time. And again the least productive was the large-group meeting, with only 46.89 percent productive time.

The five most significant meeting problems for prefixes 5-10 are as follows:

1. Side issues predominate
2. No results/follow-up
3. Objectives unclear
4. Lack of preparation
5. No agenda

Index